WEB DESIGN

a beginner's guide

2023

DOBBS MEDIA

Table of Contents

1. Learn the Basics:

a. HTML (Hypertext Markup Language):

- **What is HTML?** HTML is the backbone of web design and stands for Hypertext Markup Language. It is a markup language used to structure the content on web pages. HTML defines the structure and organization of a web page, including headings, paragraphs, lists, links, images, and more.

- **Basic HTML Structure:** An HTML document typically starts with a document type declaration (**<!DOCTYPE html>**) and contains essential elements like **<html>**, **<head>**, and **<body>**:

```html
<!DOCTYPE html>
<html>
<head>
    <title>My Web Page</title>
</head>
<body>
    <h1>Welcome to My Web Page</h1>
    <p>This is a paragraph of text.</p>
</body>
</html>
```

- **HTML Tags:** HTML uses tags to define and structure content. Common tags include:

  - **<h1>, <h2>, <h3>**: Headings

  - **<p>**: Paragraphs

  - **<a>**: Links

  - **<img>**: Images

  - **<ul>, <ol>, <li>**: Lists

  - **<div>**: Generic container

- **Attributes:** HTML tags often have attributes that provide additional information. For instance, the **<a>** tag uses the **href** attribute to specify a link's destination:

```html
<a href="https://www.example.com">Visit Example.com</a>
```

- **Semantic HTML:** It's essential to use semantic HTML tags to convey the meaning of content. For example, use **<header>, <nav>, <main>, <article>**, and **<footer>** to structure content semantically, which aids in accessibility and SEO.

b. CSS (Cascading Style Sheets):

- **What is CSS?** CSS stands for Cascading Style Sheets. It's a stylesheet language used for controlling the presentation and layout of web pages. CSS allows you to define the colors, fonts, spacing, and positioning of HTML elements.

- **Basic CSS Syntax:** CSS rules consist of selectors that target HTML elements and declaration blocks containing property-value pairs. Here's an example:

```css
CSS

h1 {
    color: blue;
    font-size: 24px;
}
```

- **Selectors:** CSS selectors determine which HTML elements the rules apply to. Common selectors include element selectors (e.g., **h1, p**), class selectors (e.g., **.classname**), and ID selectors (e.g., **#idname**).

- **Properties and Values:** CSS properties (e.g., **color, font-size, margin, padding**) specify what aspect of an element to style, while values define the style itself. Experiment with different property-value pairs to see their effects.

- **Box Model:** The CSS box model defines how elements are rendered, including content, padding, border, and margin. Understanding this model is crucial for controlling layout.

- **CSS Layout:** Learn CSS layout techniques like positioning, floating, Flexbox, and CSS Grid to create responsive and well-structured web page designs.

c. Understanding Website Concepts:

- **Hosting:**

  - Web hosting is the process of storing and serving web files on a web server. Websites need hosting to be accessible on the internet.

  - There are various types of hosting, such as shared hosting (multiple sites on one server), VPS hosting (dedicated virtual server), and dedicated hosting (an entire server for one site).

- **Domains:**

  - Domain names are human-readable website addresses (e.g., www.example.com). They are essential for users to find and access your website.

  - To use a domain, you need to register it through domain registrars and configure its DNS (Domain Name System) settings to point to your web hosting server.

- **Web Servers:**
  - A web server is software or hardware that handles requests and serves web content to users' browsers.
  - Common web server software includes Apache, Nginx, and Microsoft IIS (Internet Information Services).

- **HTTP/HTTPS:**
  - HTTP (Hypertext Transfer Protocol) and HTTPS (HTTP Secure) are communication protocols used to transmit data between web servers and browsers.
  - HTTPS, secured with SSL/TLS certificates, encrypts data for security. It's essential for protecting sensitive information and improving SEO.

By mastering these foundational aspects of web design, you'll have a solid starting point for creating well-structured and visually appealing web pages, as well as understanding the infrastructure needed to make your websites accessible to users on the internet. Continued practice and learning will help you advance your web design skills further.

2. Choose a Text Editor:

A text editor or IDE is an essential tool for web designers and developers, as it's where you write, edit, and manage your website's code and files. Here's a detailed breakdown of this step:

a. Text Editors vs. IDEs:

- **Text Editor:** A text editor is a lightweight software designed primarily for editing and managing code. Text editors are often minimalistic, offering features like syntax highlighting and customizable themes. They are known for their speed and simplicity. Examples include Sublime Text, Notepad++, and Visual Studio Code (which can be used as both a text editor and an IDE).

- **Integrated Development Environment (IDE):** An IDE is a more comprehensive software package that includes not only a text editor but also features like code debugging, version control integration, and project management tools. IDEs are often favored for larger projects or when you need a more extensive set of development features. Examples include JetBrains PhpStorm, PyCharm, and Eclipse.

b. Factors to Consider When Choosing a Text Editor or IDE:

- **Ease of Use:** Look for an editor with an intuitive interface that suits your workflow. Most modern editors offer user-friendly interfaces.

- **Syntax Highlighting:** This feature color-codes different elements of your code, making it easier to read and debug.

- **Extensions and Plugins:** Check for a robust ecosystem of extensions and plugins. These can add functionality such as auto-completion, linting, and integration with other development tools.

- **Cross-Platform Compatibility:** Choose an editor that is available for your operating system (Windows, macOS, Linux) if you work across multiple platforms.

- **Customization:** Consider whether the editor allows you to customize themes, key bindings, and other preferences to match your coding style.

- **Performance:** Ensure that the editor is responsive and doesn't slow down when working with large files or projects.

- **Community and Support:** A vibrant community and active support channels can be invaluable when you encounter issues or need help with your editor.

c. Popular Text Editors and IDEs for Web Design:

- **Visual Studio Code (VS Code):**

  - VS Code is a free, open-source code editor developed by Microsoft. It's highly extensible and has a vast marketplace of extensions, making it suitable for a wide range of programming languages and web development tasks.

- VS Code supports Git integration, debugging, and an integrated terminal.

- **Sublime Text:**

  - Sublime Text is known for its speed and elegance. It offers a distraction-free writing mode and a large library of community-created plugins.

  - Sublime Text is not free, but it has an unlimited evaluation period with occasional pop-up reminders to purchase.

- **Atom:**

  - Atom is an open-source code editor developed by GitHub. It's highly customizable and designed for web development. Atom offers a package system for adding features.

  - It's free and actively maintained by the community.

- **Brackets:**

- Brackets is an open-source code editor focused on web development. It's known for its live preview feature, which allows you to see changes in real-time as you edit your HTML and CSS.

- Brackets is lightweight and designed with web designers in mind.

- **Notepad++:**

  - Notepad++ is a free, Windows-only code editor. It's lightweight and has a range of programming language support, including HTML and CSS.

  - While it's not as feature-rich as some other editors, it's quick and easy to use.

d. Making Your Choice:

- Ultimately, the choice of a text editor or IDE comes down to personal preference and your specific needs as a web designer. Consider trying out a few different editors to see which one aligns best with your workflow and coding style.

- Many web designers start with Visual Studio Code due to its popularity, extensive extension support, and frequent updates. However, the other options mentioned also have dedicated user bases and can be excellent choices depending on your requirements.

Remember that the choice of a text editor or IDE is a valuable one, as it can significantly impact your productivity and coding experience. Take your time to explore different options and select the one that feels most comfortable and efficient for your web design projects.

3. Responsive Design:

a. What is Responsive Web Design?

- Responsive web design is an approach to web development that focuses on creating websites that adapt and respond to different screen sizes and devices. It ensures that your site looks and functions optimally on everything from large desktop monitors to smartphones and tablets.

- The key principle of responsive design is fluidity. Instead of designing separate websites for different devices, you create a single flexible design that adjusts and rearranges content based on the user's screen size and resolution.

b. Key Concepts of Responsive Design:

- **Fluid Grids:** One of the core components of responsive design is the use of fluid grids. Instead of fixed-width layouts, you define grid structures using relative units like percentages rather than fixed pixels. This allows content to expand or shrink to fit different screen sizes.

- **Flexible Images:** Images can be problematic when designing for different devices. By using CSS to set **max-width: 100%** on images, you ensure that they scale proportionally to the width of their container without breaking the layout.

- **Media Queries:** Media queries are CSS rules that apply specific styles based on the characteristics of the user's device, such as screen width, height, or orientation (landscape or portrait). These queries allow you to create breakpoints in your design where the layout or styling changes to accommodate different screen sizes.

- **Viewport Meta Tag:** Adding a viewport meta tag in your HTML **<head>** helps control the initial zoom level and scaling of your web page on mobile devices. For example:

```html
<meta name="viewport" content="width=device-width, initial-scale=1.0">
```

c. Best Practices for Responsive Design:

- **Mobile-First Approach:** Start by designing and developing for mobile devices first. This ensures that your site is optimized for the smallest screens and progressively enhanced for larger ones.

- **Use Relative Units:** Instead of fixed pixel values, use relative units like percentages or **em** for font sizes and element dimensions. This allows content to scale naturally.

- **Test Across Devices:** Regularly test your website on various devices and screen sizes to identify and address issues. Emulators and browser developer tools can help with this.

- **Optimize Images:** Compress and optimize images to reduce loading times, especially on mobile devices with slower internet connections.

- **Prioritize Content:** Consider what content is most important and ensure it remains accessible and prominent on smaller screens.

This may involve reordering elements or collapsing menus.

- **Progressive Enhancement:** Apply additional features and styling for larger screens using media queries. Progressive enhancement ensures that users with more capable devices get an enhanced experience without excluding those with basic ones.

d. Tools and Frameworks:

- Several CSS frameworks like Bootstrap and Foundation provide responsive design grids and components out of the box. These frameworks can be helpful for beginners as they streamline the responsive design process.

e. The Importance of Responsive Design:

- Mobile devices have become the primary way people access the internet. Ignoring responsive design can lead to a poor user experience for a significant portion of your audience.

- Google and other search engines prioritize mobile-friendly websites in their rankings, making responsive design crucial for SEO.

- Responsive design demonstrates a commitment to user experience, accessibility, and adaptability, which can positively impact your website's reputation and user engagement.

In conclusion, responsive web design is a fundamental skill for web designers and developers. It ensures that your website can reach and engage users across various devices, leading to better user experiences and improved search engine rankings. Understanding the principles and best practices of responsive design is essential for modern web development.

4. Typography:

a. Typography Principles:

- **Typography is the art and technique of arranging type to make written language readable and visually appealing. In web design, it involves selecting fonts, font sizes, line spacing, and other text-related properties to enhance the overall design and readability of your website.

- **Readability:** The primary goal of typography is to ensure that the content is easy to read. This involves selecting fonts and text sizes that are comfortable for users to read on various screen sizes and resolutions.

- **Hierarchy:** Typography helps establish a visual hierarchy on your website. By using different fonts, font weights, sizes, and styles (such as italics and bold), you can guide users' attention to important content like headings, subheadings, and calls to action.

- **Consistency:** Consistency in typography throughout your website creates a cohesive and professional appearance. Consistent font choices and styling make it easier for users to navigate your site and understand its structure.

- **Alignment and Spacing:** Proper alignment and spacing between text elements contribute to readability and aesthetics. Justified text alignment, adequate line spacing (leading), and appropriate margins all play a role in creating a visually pleasing layout.

b. Choosing Fonts:

- **Font Categories:** Fonts can be broadly categorized into serif, sans-serif, and display fonts.

  - **Serif Fonts:** These fonts have decorative lines or strokes at the ends of their characters (e.g., Times New Roman). They often convey a sense of tradition and formality.

  - **Sans-serif Fonts:** These fonts lack the decorative lines and are often perceived as modern and clean (e.g., Arial, Helvetica). They are commonly used for web content.

- **Display Fonts:** These fonts are unique and eye-catching but are typically used sparingly for headings and decorative elements.

- **Font Pairing:** It's common to pair fonts to create visual contrast and hierarchy. A common practice is to pair a sans-serif font with a serif font, or combine fonts with different weights (e.g., a bold header with a regular body text).

- **Legibility:** Prioritize legibility when choosing fonts. Ensure that the fonts you select are easy to read on screens and in different font sizes.

- **Web-Safe Fonts:** While web design allows for a wide range of fonts, it's essential to consider web-safe fonts that are universally available on various devices and browsers to maintain consistent rendering.

c. Using Fonts Effectively:

- **Font Sizes:** Font size is crucial for readability. Use a responsive approach by setting font sizes in relative units like **em** or **rem** to ensure text scales appropriately on different devices.

- **Line Spacing (Leading):** Adequate line spacing between lines of text improves readability. A general rule is to set line height at 1.5 times the font size.

- **Text Formatting:** Use italics, bold, and underline sparingly to emphasize text. Be consistent in your formatting choices.

- **White Space:** Proper use of white space (blank areas around text) helps readers focus on content. Avoid overcrowding text and maintain a comfortable line width.

- **Color Contrast:** Ensure that text has sufficient contrast with the background to make it easily readable. Follow accessibility guidelines for text and background color combinations.

- **Responsive Typography:** Implement responsive typography by using media queries to adjust font sizes and styles based on screen sizes and orientations.

d. Tools for Typography:

- **Google Fonts:** Google Fonts offers a vast collection of free web fonts that you can easily embed in your web pages.

- **Adobe Typekit:** Adobe Typekit provides access to a library of high-quality fonts for web and desktop use.

- **Font Squirrel:** Font Squirrel offers a collection of free fonts that can be used for web projects, and it provides font conversion tools.

- **Typography.io:** This tool helps you select font pairings and provides code snippets for implementing them.

e. Testing and Feedback:

- Always test your typography choices on various devices and screen sizes to ensure readability and visual appeal.

- Seek feedback from others, especially if you're not a trained graphic designer, to get insights into how your typography choices are perceived by users.

Typography is a critical element of web design that can greatly influence how users engage with your content. By understanding typography principles and making informed choices about fonts, sizes, and styles, you can create web designs that are not only visually appealing but also highly readable and user-friendly.

5. Color Theory:

a. Basics of Color Theory:

- **Color theory** is the study of how colors interact and the principles behind combining them effectively to create visually pleasing designs. In web design, understanding color theory is essential for creating harmonious and engaging websites.

- **Color Wheel:** The color wheel is a visual representation of colors arranged in a circular format. It's a useful tool for understanding color relationships. The primary color wheel consists of three main color categories:

    - **Primary Colors:** Red, blue, and yellow. These colors cannot be created by mixing other colors.

    - **Secondary Colors:** Green, orange, and purple. These colors are created by mixing two primary colors.

    - **Tertiary Colors:** These are created by mixing a primary color with a neighboring secondary color (e.g., red-orange, yellow-green).

- **Color Properties:** Understanding color properties is crucial:

    - **Hue:** Hue is the actual color name (e.g., red, blue, green).

    - **Saturation:** Saturation refers to the intensity or purity of a color. Fully saturated colors are vivid, while desaturated colors are more muted.

    - **Brightness or Value:** This measures the lightness or darkness of a color. It determines how a color appears in different lighting conditions.

b. Creating Harmonious Color Schemes:

- **Color Harmony:** Achieving color harmony means selecting colors that work well together and create a pleasing visual experience. There are several color harmony models to consider:

    - **Analogous:** Analogous color schemes use colors that are adjacent to each other on the color wheel. For example, blue, green, and teal form an analogous scheme. It provides a sense of harmony and unity.

- **Complementary:** Complementary colors are opposite each other on the color wheel, such as red and green or blue and orange. This scheme creates strong contrast and vibrancy.

- **Triadic:** A triadic color scheme uses three evenly spaced colors on the color wheel. For example, red, yellow, and blue form a triadic scheme. It's vibrant and balanced.

- **Monochromatic:** Monochromatic color schemes use variations of a single color, such as different shades of blue. It creates a harmonious and elegant look.

- **Contrast:** Ensuring sufficient contrast between text and background colors is essential for readability. You can use tools like the Web Content Accessibility Guidelines (WCAG) to determine adequate contrast ratios for accessibility.

c. Psychological Effects of Color:

- Colors can evoke specific emotions and perceptions. For example:

    - **Red:** Often associated with passion, energy, and urgency.

    - **Blue:** Conveys calmness, trust, and professionalism.

    - **Yellow:** Represents positivity, happiness, and warmth.

    - **Green:** Symbolizes growth, nature, and health.

    - **Purple:** Suggests luxury, creativity, and sophistication.

- Consider your target audience and the emotional impact you want to achieve when selecting colors for your website.

d. Tools and Resources:

- **Color Picker Tools:** Use color picker tools like Adobe Color Wheel, Coolors, or Paletton to explore and select colors for your website.

- **Color Scheme Generators:** Tools like Adobe Color Wheel and Coolors can generate color schemes based on your preferences.

- **Color Palette Inspiration:** Websites like Dribbble, Behance, and Pinterest can be excellent sources of color palette inspiration.

e. Testing and Feedback:

- Before finalizing your color scheme, test it on different devices and monitor how it looks in various lighting conditions.

- Seek feedback from colleagues or users to ensure that your color choices resonate with your target audience and convey the intended message.

In conclusion, mastering color theory is crucial for creating visually appealing and effective web designs. Understanding the principles of the color wheel, color properties, harmony models, and the psychological impact of colors will help you make informed decisions about color selection and create websites that engage and resonate with your audience.

6. Layout and Grids:

a. Layout Principles:

- **Layout** in web design refers to the arrangement and positioning of elements on a web page. An effective layout:

  - Guides the user's eye smoothly through the content.

  - Prioritizes and highlights essential information.

  - Provides a logical flow and hierarchy to the content.

  - Enhances visual appeal and user experience.

- **Key Layout Principles:**

  - **Balance:** Achieving visual balance ensures that elements are distributed evenly across the page, creating a harmonious composition.

- **Proximity:** Group related elements together to signify their connection and separate unrelated items.

- **Contrast:** Use contrasting elements (e.g., color, size, typography) to draw attention to important content.

- **Alignment:** Consistent alignment of elements, whether left, right, center, or justified, provides a structured appearance.

- **Whitespace:** Proper use of whitespace (also known as negative space) around elements improves readability and enhances aesthetics.

b. Grid Systems:

- **Grid systems** are a structured framework of rows and columns used to align and organize content on a web page. Grids provide a systematic approach to layout design, making it easier to create consistent and visually pleasing designs.

- **Benefits of Using Grids:**

  - Ensures alignment and consistency in design.

  - Facilitates responsive design, adapting layouts to different screen sizes.

  - Speeds up the design process by providing a structured framework.

  - Enhances readability and usability by creating a logical flow of content.

c. Types of Grids:

- **Symmetrical Grids:** Symmetrical grids divide the layout into equal halves or thirds, creating a balanced and formal appearance. They are often used for corporate or information-focused websites.

- **Asymmetrical Grids:** Asymmetrical grids use uneven divisions to create dynamic and visually interesting layouts. They are commonly employed for creative and artistic websites.

- **Modular Grids:** Modular grids break the layout into a series of modules or containers, allowing for flexibility and adaptability in design. They are useful for content-heavy websites.

- **Column Grids:** Column grids are a popular choice for web design, dividing the layout into columns. They provide a flexible and responsive structure for arranging content.

d. Responsive Grid Design:

- With the proliferation of various devices and screen sizes, responsive web design has become essential. Responsive grids adapt to different screen sizes and orientations, ensuring a consistent and user-friendly experience on desktops, tablets, and smartphones.

- Techniques such as CSS Grid and Flexbox have made it easier to create responsive grid layouts. Media queries are used to adjust grid layouts at specific breakpoints to optimize the user experience on various devices.

e. Tools and Resources:

- **Grid Generators:** There are various online grid generators and frameworks like Bootstrap,

Foundation, and Grid by Example that can help you create responsive grid layouts efficiently.

- **Design Software:** Adobe XD, Sketch, and Figma are design software tools that offer grid-based layout capabilities and allow you to design and prototype grid-based layouts.

f. Testing and Feedback:

- Always test your grid layouts on different devices and screen sizes to ensure that they adapt and function correctly in various scenarios.

- Gather feedback from users to identify any usability issues or design improvements related to your grid layout.

In summary, layout and grid systems are foundational elements of web design that provide structure and organization to your web pages. By applying layout principles and using grid systems effectively, you can create organized, visually appealing, and user-friendly web designs that adapt seamlessly to different devices and screen sizes.

7. Web Accessibility in Web Design:

a. Understanding Web Accessibility:

- **Web accessibility** refers to the practice of designing and developing websites and web applications in a way that makes them usable and accessible to people with disabilities. The primary goal of web accessibility is to ensure that all users, regardless of their abilities or disabilities, can perceive, understand, navigate, and interact with web content.

- **Types of Disabilities:** Web accessibility addresses a wide range of disabilities, including but not limited to:

  - Visual impairments (e.g., blindness, low vision)

  - Hearing impairments (e.g., deafness, hard of hearing)

  - Motor impairments (e.g., difficulty using a mouse)

- Cognitive impairments (e.g., dyslexia, learning disabilities)

b. Web Content Accessibility Guidelines (WCAG):

- The **Web Content Accessibility Guidelines (WCAG)** are a set of internationally recognized standards developed by the World Wide Web Consortium (W3C) to guide web developers and designers in creating accessible web content. WCAG outlines four key principles:

  - **Perceivable:** Information and user interface components must be presentable to users in ways they can perceive. This involves using alternative text for images, providing captions for multimedia, and ensuring sufficient contrast between text and background.

  - **Operable:** User interface components and navigation must be operable. This includes keyboard navigation, providing skip navigation links, and ensuring that all interactive elements are accessible via a keyboard.

- **Understandable:** Information and operation of the user interface must be understandable. This involves clear and concise content, predictable navigation, and avoiding content that flashes or moves excessively.

- **Robust:** Content must be robust enough to be reliably interpreted by a wide variety of user agents, including assistive technologies. This means following web standards, using semantic HTML, and testing with multiple browsers and devices.

c. Practical Implementation:

- **Semantic HTML:** Using semantic HTML elements (e.g., **<header>**, **<nav>**, **<main>**, **<article>**) provides a clear structure to your content, making it easier for screen readers and other assistive technologies to interpret.

- **Alternative Text:** Include descriptive alternative text (alt text) for images and other non-text content. Alt text should convey the content and purpose of the element.

- **Keyboard Accessibility:** Ensure that all interactive elements, such as forms and buttons, are navigable and usable with a keyboard. Implement focus styles to indicate the currently focused element.

- **Contrast and Color:** Maintain sufficient contrast between text and background colors to improve readability for users with visual impairments. Avoid relying solely on color to convey information.

- **Transcripts and Captions:** Provide transcripts for audio content and captions for video content. This benefits users with hearing impairments and those who prefer text-based content.

- **Testing:** Regularly test your website with assistive technologies such as screen readers (e.g., JAWS, VoiceOver) and keyboard navigation. Additionally, use automated testing tools and browser extensions like axe and Wave to identify accessibility issues.

d. Accessibility Resources:

- The **W3C Web Accessibility Initiative (WAI)** provides extensive resources, including the full WCAG guidelines, techniques, and best practices.

- The **WebAIM (Web Accessibility In Mind)** organization offers guides, training, and tools for web accessibility testing and implementation.

- **ARIA (Accessible Rich Internet Applications)** is a set of attributes that can be added to HTML elements to improve the accessibility of dynamic content and web applications.

e. The Legal and Ethical Importance:

- Web accessibility is not just a best practice; it can also have legal implications. Many countries have laws and regulations that require websites to be accessible to people with disabilities.

- Beyond legal requirements, it is also an ethical responsibility to ensure that everyone, regardless of their abilities, can access and use the information and services provided on the web.

In conclusion, web accessibility is a critical aspect of web design that ensures equal access and usability for all users. By following the WCAG guidelines and best practices, web designers and developers can create inclusive web experiences that benefit a diverse audience and comply with legal and ethical obligations.

8. Navigation:

a. Importance of Navigation:

- **Navigation** on a website refers to the structure and organization of links and menus that allow users to move around and access different parts of the site. Effective navigation is essential because:

  - It helps users find information quickly and easily.

  - It enhances user satisfaction by simplifying the user's journey.

  - It contributes to a website's overall usability and accessibility.

  - It influences how users perceive and interact with your site.

b. Types of Navigation:

- **Primary Navigation:** This is the main menu typically found at the top of a webpage. It provides access to essential sections or pages of the site, often categorized into sections like "Home," "About," "Services," and "Contact."

- **Secondary Navigation:** Secondary navigation menus are used to provide links to pages that are important but not as central as those in the primary menu. These are often found in sidebars or footers.

- **Breadcrumbs:** Breadcrumbs are a trail of links that show the user's current location within the site's hierarchy. They help users understand where they are and navigate backward if needed.

- **Hamburger Menu:** Common on mobile and responsive websites, the hamburger menu is an icon (usually three horizontal lines) that, when clicked, reveals a hidden navigation menu. It helps save screen space on smaller devices.

- **Tabs:** Tabs are a type of navigation used to switch between different sections or views within a single page. They are often used for organizing content on product pages, dashboards, or applications.

c. Best Practices for Navigation Design:

- **Clear Labeling:** Use concise and descriptive labels for navigation links. Avoid vague terms like "Click Here" and instead use contextually relevant labels like "View Services" or "Read Blog."

- **Consistency:** Keep navigation elements consistent throughout your website. Users should easily recognize and understand how to navigate, regardless of the page they are on.

- **Prioritization:** Prioritize links in your primary navigation menu based on user needs and the site's goals. Highlight the most important pages prominently.

- **Limited Choices:** Avoid overwhelming users with too many navigation options. Aim for a streamlined menu with the most critical links and use secondary menus or dropdowns for additional items.

- **Accessibility:** Ensure that navigation is accessible to all users, including those with disabilities. Use semantic HTML, provide keyboard navigation support, and ensure focus styles are visible.

- **Mobile Responsiveness:** Test and optimize navigation for mobile devices. Consider mobile-specific navigation patterns, such as the hamburger menu, to save space.

- **Search Functionality:** Include a search bar for users who prefer searching for content. Make sure it is prominently placed and functional.

- **User Testing:** Conduct user testing to gather feedback on your navigation. Observe how users interact with your site and make improvements based on their feedback.

d. User-Centered Design:

- Keep the user in mind when designing navigation. Think about their goals, the information they seek, and how they might want to move through your website.

- Conduct user research, such as user interviews or surveys, to understand their preferences and pain points related to navigation.

e. Information Architecture:

- Information architecture is the process of organizing and structuring content to make it easily navigable. It involves creating sitemaps, content hierarchies, and taxonomies.

- Plan your site's information architecture carefully to ensure that content is logically organized and accessible.

f. Testing and Iteration:

- Regularly test your website's navigation with real users to identify issues and gather insights for improvements. Use tools like heatmaps and click-tracking to analyze user behavior.

- Continuously iterate and refine your navigation based on user feedback and data-driven insights.

In conclusion, effective navigation is crucial for improving user experience on your website. By following best practices, considering user needs, and prioritizing clarity and accessibility, you can design intuitive navigation menus and site structures that enhance user satisfaction and help visitors find the content they seek efficiently.

9. User Interface (UI) and User Experience (UX):

a. Understanding UI and UX:

- **User Interface (UI)** refers to the graphical layout and elements of a website, which users interact with directly. It includes visual elements like buttons, forms, menus, and the overall look and feel of the site.

- **User Experience (UX)** encompasses the overall experience that users have while interacting with your website. It considers aspects such as ease of use, accessibility, efficiency, and user satisfaction.

b. UI Principles:

- **Clarity:** A clear and well-organized UI is essential. Elements should be logically placed and labeled. Users should quickly understand how to navigate and interact with the site.

- **Consistency:** Maintain consistency in design elements, such as fonts, colors, and buttons, throughout your website. Consistency helps users build a mental model of your site's functionality.

- **Feedback:** Provide feedback for user actions. For example, when a user submits a form, display a confirmation message. Feedback helps users understand that their actions have been acknowledged.

- **Simplicity:** Keep the UI simple and avoid clutter. Remove unnecessary elements and features that may overwhelm users.

- **Hierarchy:** Use visual hierarchy to guide users through your content. Larger fonts, bold text, and contrasting colors can be used to emphasize important elements.

- **User-Centered Design:** Design with the user in mind. Understand your target audience, their needs, and their preferences. Conduct user testing and gather feedback to make informed design decisions.

- **Mobile Responsiveness:** Ensure that your UI is responsive and works well on various devices and screen sizes. Mobile users should have a seamless experience.

c. UX Principles:

- **User Research:** Conduct user research to understand your target audience's needs, behaviors, and pain points. Use this information to inform your design decisions.

- **Usability:** Prioritize usability by making it easy for users to accomplish tasks and find information. Use clear navigation, intuitive forms, and straightforward workflows.

- **Accessibility:** Ensure that your website is accessible to all users, including those with disabilities. Follow WCAG guidelines to make your site inclusive.

- **Performance:** Optimize website performance by minimizing loading times. Users are more likely to abandon a site that takes too long to load.

- **Content Strategy:** Develop a content strategy that provides valuable and relevant information to your users. Content should be well-organized and easy to digest.

- **A/B Testing:** Conduct A/B testing to experiment with different design elements and features. Test variations to determine which ones result in better user engagement and conversions.

- **User Feedback:** Encourage and collect user feedback to continuously improve your website. Feedback can reveal issues and opportunities for enhancement.

d. UI/UX Tools:

- Several tools are available to aid in UI and UX design, such as wireframing tools like Balsamiq and Figma, prototyping tools like Adobe XD and Sketch, and usability testing tools like UsabilityHub and Optimal Workshop.

e. The UX/UI Process:

- The UI/UX design process typically involves stages like research, wireframing, prototyping, testing, and implementation. It's an iterative process that requires ongoing refinement based on user feedback and data analysis.

f. Testing and Iteration:

- Regularly test your UI/UX with real users to identify usability issues and gather insights for improvements.

- Iterate on your design based on user feedback and data-driven insights to continually enhance the user experience.

In conclusion, UI and UX are critical components of web design, as they directly impact how users perceive and interact with your website. By following UI and UX principles, conducting user research, and continuously iterating on your design, you can create user-friendly websites that meet the needs of your audience and drive positive user experiences.

10. Coding Practice:

a. Why is Coding Practice Important:

- Coding practice is crucial for web designers and developers for several reasons:

  - **Skill Improvement:** Regular practice helps you become more proficient in coding languages like HTML, CSS, JavaScript, and more. It builds muscle memory and familiarity with the syntax.

  - **Problem-Solving:** Coding often involves complex problem-solving. Practicing coding challenges and projects hones your ability to think critically and find efficient solutions.

  - **Creativity:** Coding is a creative endeavor. Practice allows you to experiment with new ideas, design concepts, and functionality.

  - **Keeping Up with Trends:** The web development landscape is ever-evolving. Regular practice helps you stay up-to-date with the latest tools, frameworks, and best practices.

b. Tips for Effective Coding Practice:

- **Set Clear Goals:** Define specific coding goals for each practice session. For example, you might aim to build a simple webpage, create a responsive layout, or implement a particular JavaScript feature.

- **Start Small:** If you're new to coding, begin with small projects. Gradually increase the complexity as you become more comfortable. It's like building a foundation before constructing a skyscraper.

- **Work on Real Projects:** Practical experience is invaluable. Try building real-world projects or replicating existing websites to learn how different elements come together.

- **Learn from Others:** Analyze and study well-structured code from experienced developers. Reading code from others can teach you best practices and new techniques.

- **Practice Algorithms:** Algorithm challenges, like those on platforms like LeetCode or CodeSignal, help improve your problem-solving skills and algorithmic thinking.

- **Stay Organized:** Organize your code by using version control systems like Git and GitHub. This helps you track changes and collaborate with others.

- **Get Feedback:** Seek feedback from peers or mentors on your code. Constructive criticism can help you identify areas for improvement.

c. Coding Tools and Resources:

- **Code Editors:** Choose a code editor that suits your workflow. Popular options include Visual Studio Code, Sublime Text, Atom, and JetBrains WebStorm.

- **Online Learning Platforms:** Platforms like Codecademy, freeCodeCamp, Coursera, and Udacity offer interactive coding exercises and projects.

- **Tutorials and Documentation:** Refer to official documentation for programming languages, frameworks, and libraries. Additionally, follow online tutorials and guides to build practical skills.

- **Code Repositories:** GitHub is a valuable resource for finding open-source projects to contribute to and exploring code samples.

d. Coding Challenges and Exercises:

- Leverage coding challenges and exercises to practice and refine your coding skills. Websites like HackerRank, Codewars, and Exercism offer a wide range of coding challenges in different languages and difficulty levels.

- Participate in coding competitions and hackathons to challenge yourself and learn from others.

e. Portfolio Building:

- As you practice, consider building a portfolio of your projects. A portfolio showcases your skills and work to potential employers or clients.

- Include personal projects, contributions to open-source projects, and any freelance work you've done in your portfolio.

f. Collaborative Projects:

- Collaborating on projects with other developers can be a valuable learning experience. It exposes you to different coding styles and approaches.

- Platforms like GitHub facilitate collaboration on open-source projects. Contribute to projects you're passionate about or find interesting.

g. Staying Updated:

- Web development technologies are constantly evolving. Stay updated with industry news, blogs, and tutorials to ensure you're aware of the latest trends and best practices.

h. Time Management:

- Allocate dedicated time for coding practice in your schedule. Consistency is key to making progress.

- Consider setting coding goals for the week or month to track your improvement.

In conclusion, coding practice is an essential part of becoming a skilled web designer or developer. Regularly working on coding challenges, projects, and exercises not only strengthens your skills but also fosters creativity and problem-solving abilities. By setting goals, staying organized, and seeking feedback, you can make the most of your coding practice sessions and continually advance your abilities in web development.

11. Frameworks and Libraries:

a. Understanding Frameworks and Libraries:

- **Frameworks** and **libraries** are pre-written code collections that provide reusable components, templates, and functionalities for web development. While they serve similar purposes, there are subtle differences:

  - **Frameworks:** Frameworks are comprehensive, all-in-one packages that dictate the overall structure and organization of your web application. They often come with built-in tools, architectural patterns, and predefined workflows. Frameworks are opinionated and provide a strict structure to follow. Examples include Angular, React, and Vue.js for JavaScript, and Ruby on Rails for server-side development.

  - **Libraries:** Libraries are more focused and modular. They offer specific functionalities or components that you can incorporate into your project as needed. Libraries are flexible, allowing you to use them alongside other tools and frameworks. Examples include jQuery for JavaScript, Bootstrap and Foundation for CSS and front-end development, and Flask for Python-based server-side development.

b. Advantages of Using Frameworks and Libraries:

- **Productivity:** Frameworks and libraries come with pre-built components and functionalities, saving you time and effort. You don't need to reinvent the wheel for common tasks.

- **Consistency:** Frameworks enforce best practices and coding standards, ensuring a consistent and maintainable codebase.

- **Community Support:** Popular frameworks and libraries often have large and active communities. You can find extensive documentation, tutorials, and support forums to help you overcome challenges.

- **Scalability:** Frameworks and libraries are designed to handle complex applications. They provide a structured architecture that can scale as your project grows.

- **Cross-Browser Compatibility:** Many libraries and frameworks address cross-browser compatibility issues, reducing the need for extensive browser-specific testing.

- **Security:** Frameworks often have built-in security features and protection against common vulnerabilities, such as SQL injection and cross-site scripting (XSS).

c. Popular Frameworks and Libraries:

Front-end Frameworks and Libraries:

- **Bootstrap:** Bootstrap is a widely-used front-end framework that provides a responsive grid system, pre-designed UI components, and CSS styles. It simplifies the process of creating mobile-friendly websites.

- **Foundation:** Foundation is another responsive front-end framework with a modular approach.

It offers customizable grid systems, typography, and UI components.

- **jQuery:** jQuery is a JavaScript library that simplifies DOM manipulation, event handling, and asynchronous operations. It makes it easier to work with JavaScript across different browsers.

JavaScript Frameworks:

- **React:** Developed by Facebook, React is a JavaScript library for building user interfaces. It follows a component-based architecture and is known for its performance and reusability.

- **Angular:** Developed by Google, Angular is a comprehensive front-end framework that provides a full suite of tools for building web applications. It follows the MVC (Model-View-Controller) architecture.

- **Vue.js:** Vue.js is a progressive JavaScript framework that is easy to integrate into existing projects. It offers a flexible and approachable way to build user interfaces.

Server-side Frameworks:

- **Express.js:** Express.js is a minimal and flexible Node.js web application framework that simplifies the creation of server-side applications and APIs.

- **Ruby on Rails:** Ruby on Rails (often referred to as Rails) is a robust server-side framework for building web applications using the Ruby programming language. It emphasizes convention over configuration.

- **Django:** Django is a high-level Python web framework that encourages rapid development and clean, pragmatic design. It comes with an admin panel for easy content management.

d. Considerations When Choosing Frameworks and Libraries:

- **Project Requirements:** Select frameworks and libraries based on the specific needs of your project. Some frameworks are better suited for single-page applications, while others are more suitable for content-driven websites.

- **Learning Curve:** Consider the learning curve associated with a framework or library. Some may have steeper learning curves than others, depending on your prior experience and familiarity with the technology stack.

- **Community and Documentation:** Ensure that the framework or library has an active community and comprehensive documentation. Community support is valuable when you encounter issues or need guidance.

- **Longevity and Maintenance:** Choose technologies that are actively maintained and have a track record of longevity. You don't want to invest time and effort into a tool that becomes obsolete.

e. Best Practices with Frameworks and Libraries:

- **Customization:** While frameworks provide default styles and components, it's essential to customize them to match your project's unique design and branding.

- **Version Control:** Keep frameworks and libraries up to date to benefit from bug fixes, security patches, and new features.

- **Performance Optimization:** Use tools like bundlers (e.g., Webpack) and code splitting to optimize the loading and performance of your web applications.

- **Testing:** Conduct thorough testing, including unit testing and integration testing, to ensure that the framework or library doesn't introduce unexpected issues.

- **Security:** Follow security best practices and regularly review the security of the frameworks and libraries you use. Update dependencies to patch known vulnerabilities.

f. Learning and Practicing with Frameworks and Libraries:

- To learn how to use frameworks and libraries effectively, follow official documentation, tutorials, and online courses. Many educational platforms offer courses on popular frameworks and libraries.

- Practice by building projects that incorporate the chosen framework or library. Start with small projects and gradually work your way up to more complex applications.

g. Staying Informed:

- Stay updated with the latest releases and updates of the frameworks and libraries you use. Subscribe to mailing lists, follow official blogs, and join relevant communities to stay informed.

In summary, frameworks and libraries are valuable tools in web development that can significantly expedite the development process, enhance code quality, and provide solutions to common challenges. When choosing a framework or library, consider your project's requirements, learning curve, community support, and long-term maintenance. Regular practice and continuous learning are key to effectively utilizing these tools in your web design and development projects.

12. Responsive Web Design Frameworks:

a. Importance of Responsive Design:

- **Responsive web design** is the practice of creating websites that adapt and respond to different screen sizes and devices. It ensures that users have a consistent and user-friendly experience, whether they are accessing your site on a desktop computer, tablet, or smartphone.

- With the increasing diversity of devices and screen resolutions, responsive design is crucial for reaching a broader audience and improving user engagement.

b. CSS Frameworks for Responsive Design:

- **Flexbox:** Flexbox, short for "Flexible Box Layout," is a CSS layout model that simplifies the creation of complex and responsive layouts. It allows you to distribute space within a container and align items in a way that accommodates different screen sizes.

- Key Features of Flexbox:

  - Direction-Agnostic: You can create both row-based and column-based layouts.

  - Dynamic Sizing: Elements can grow or shrink to fit the available space.

  - Content Alignment: Easily align content both horizontally and vertically.

  - Order Control: Reorder elements without changing the HTML structure.

- **CSS Grid:** CSS Grid is another CSS layout model that provides a grid-based approach to creating responsive layouts. It allows you to define rows and columns, making it ideal for creating grid-based designs with precision.

  - Key Features of CSS Grid:

    - Two-Dimensional Layout: You can create both row and column layouts simultaneously.

- Automatic Sizing: Grid items can automatically adjust their size based on content or available space.

- Control Over Alignment: Precisely control the alignment of items within the grid.

- Grid Template Areas: Define named areas for different sections of your layout.

c. Best Practices for Using Flexbox and CSS Grid:

- **Start with a Mobile-First Approach:** Begin designing your layout for mobile devices and then progressively enhance it for larger screens. This approach ensures a strong foundation for responsive design.

- **Use Media Queries:** Employ media queries in your CSS to apply specific styles and layout adjustments based on screen size breakpoints.

- **Combine Flexbox and CSS Grid:** Flexbox is great for handling one-dimensional layouts, while CSS

Grid excels in two-dimensional layouts. You can use both techniques in the same project for maximum flexibility.

- **Test on Various Devices:** Regularly test your responsive designs on different devices and screen sizes to ensure they work as intended.

- **Content-First Design:** Focus on the content and the user experience. Prioritize content that's most critical for users on smaller screens and progressively enhance it for larger screens.

- **Browser Compatibility:** While Flexbox and CSS Grid are well-supported in modern browsers, ensure graceful degradation or use fallbacks for older or less capable browsers.

d. Responsive Frameworks vs. CSS Grid/Flexbox:

- Responsive web design frameworks like Bootstrap and Foundation provide a higher-level solution, including pre-designed UI components, grid systems, and responsive utilities. They are ideal for rapid development but may have a learning curve.

- CSS Grid and Flexbox offer more control over layout design but require a deeper understanding of CSS. You can use these alongside or instead of responsive frameworks, depending on your project's needs.

e. Learning Resources:

- Tutorials and documentation for Flexbox and CSS Grid are widely available online. Start with official resources and follow up with community-contributed tutorials and examples.

- Online courses and interactive coding platforms often offer in-depth lessons on using Flexbox and CSS Grid for responsive design.

f. Continuous Practice:

- Responsive design is an ongoing process. As you learn and become more proficient with Flexbox and CSS Grid, practice by building a variety of layouts and applications to solidify your skills.

In conclusion, responsive web design frameworks like Flexbox and CSS Grid are powerful tools for creating adaptive and user-friendly layouts. These frameworks, along with best practices such as mobile-first design and thorough testing, ensure that your websites look and function well across a wide range of devices and screen sizes. Continuous practice and exploration of responsive design techniques will help you master these tools and enhance your web development skills.

13. Content Management Systems (CMS):

a. Understanding CMS:

- A **Content Management System (CMS)** is a software platform that allows users to create, manage, and publish digital content on the web without needing extensive technical knowledge. CMS platforms streamline the process of website creation and content updates.

- Key features of CMS platforms include content editing, media management, user access control, templates/themes for design consistency, and plugins/extensions for added functionality.

b. Popular CMS Platforms:

- **WordPress:** WordPress is one of the most widely used CMS platforms globally. It's known for its user-friendly interface and extensive ecosystem of themes and plugins. WordPress is highly customizable, making it suitable for various types of websites, from blogs to e-commerce stores.

- **Joomla:** Joomla is a versatile CMS that strikes a balance between ease of use and customization. It offers robust user management, content organization, and multilingual capabilities. Joomla is often chosen for community websites, e-commerce, and corporate portals.

- **Drupal:** Drupal is a powerful and highly customizable CMS favored for its scalability and security features. It excels in managing complex content structures and is often used for large-scale websites, government portals, and enterprise solutions.

c. Benefits of Learning CMS Platforms:

- **Efficiency:** CMS platforms simplify website creation and content management, reducing the time and effort required for development and updates.

- **Accessibility:** CMS platforms make it possible for non-technical users to manage and publish content, democratizing web publishing.

- **Customization:** While CMS platforms offer pre-built themes and plugins, they also allow for extensive customization, catering to specific design and functionality requirements.

- **Community and Support:** Popular CMS platforms have active user communities, providing access to forums, documentation, and support resources.

- **Scalability:** CMS platforms can handle websites of varying sizes and complexity, from personal blogs to large e-commerce sites.

d. Learning CMS Platforms:

- **WordPress:** To learn WordPress, start with the official WordPress.org website, which offers comprehensive documentation and tutorials. You can also explore online courses and community forums. Setting up a local development environment using tools like XAMPP or using hosting services that offer one-click WordPress installations can help you practice.

- **Joomla:** Joomla's official website provides documentation and tutorials for beginners. Joomla also offers a beginner's guide to help you get started. Additionally, online courses and Joomla-focused forums are available for further learning.

- **Drupal:** Drupal.org provides detailed documentation and guides for learning Drupal. The Drupalize.Me platform offers a comprehensive library of Drupal tutorials, including video lessons. Setting up a local development environment for Drupal is a common practice for hands-on learning.

e. Practical Benefits:

- As a web designer or developer, knowing how to work with CMS platforms can be beneficial in various ways:

  - **Client Projects:** Many clients prefer to manage their websites' content using a

CMS. Proficiency in CMS platforms makes you a more attractive service provider.

- **Efficiency:** CMS platforms speed up the website development process, allowing you to take on more projects.

- **Diversification:** Learning different CMS platforms expands your skill set and opens up opportunities to work on a wider range of projects.

f. Keeping Up-to-Date:

- CMS platforms are regularly updated to improve security, performance, and features. It's important to stay current with the latest versions and best practices for each CMS platform you work with.

g. Choosing the Right CMS:

- The choice of CMS platform depends on the specific needs of a project. Consider factors like scalability, customization requirements, and the technical proficiency of the end-users when selecting a CMS.

h. Experiment and Build Projects:

- The best way to learn CMS platforms is through hands-on practice. Start by creating personal websites or small projects to experiment and apply what you've learned.

In conclusion, learning popular CMS platforms like WordPress, Joomla, and Drupal can significantly enhance your efficiency as a web designer or developer. These platforms provide a user-friendly way to create and manage websites, and they are widely used across the industry. By becoming proficient in CMS platforms, you can offer clients more versatile solutions, streamline your workflow, and expand your opportunities in the web development field.

14. Web Design Tools:

a. Purpose of Web Design Tools:

- Web design tools are software applications designed specifically for creating and designing websites, web applications, and user interfaces. They serve several key purposes:

    - **Mockup and Wireframe Creation:** These tools allow designers to create static representations (wireframes) or high-fidelity visual designs (mockups) of web pages or applications.

    - **Prototype Development:** They enable the creation of interactive prototypes, which simulate the user experience and functionality of a website or app.

    - **Collaboration:** Design tools often support collaboration features, allowing designers to work with developers and other stakeholders on a project.

    - **Design Consistency:** They help maintain design consistency throughout a project by providing design assets, style guides, and reusable components.

b. Popular Web Design Tools:

- **Adobe XD:** Adobe XD is a versatile design and prototyping tool that's part of the Adobe Creative Cloud suite. It's known for its integration with other Adobe products, making it easy to work with Photoshop and Illustrator files. Adobe XD offers robust design and prototyping capabilities.

- **Sketch:** Sketch is a macOS-exclusive design tool that's highly regarded for its simplicity and efficiency. It's known for its vector-based workflow and a thriving ecosystem of plugins and integrations. Sketch is popular among UI and UX designers.

- **Figma:** Figma is a web-based design and prototyping tool that supports real-time collaboration and cross-platform compatibility (macOS, Windows, and Linux). It's accessible from any browser and offers features for both design and collaboration.

- **InVision:** While InVision is primarily a prototyping and collaboration tool, it also offers design capabilities. Designers can create interactive prototypes and collaborate with developers and stakeholders using InVision.

- **Adobe Photoshop and Illustrator:** These classic Adobe design tools are still widely used for web design. Photoshop is known for its image editing capabilities, while Illustrator excels at vector graphics.

c. Key Features of Web Design Tools:

- **Artboards:** Design tools often use artboards to represent individual screens or pages within a project, allowing designers to work on different parts of a website or app in one file.

- **Vector Graphics:** Tools like Sketch and Illustrator use vector graphics, which allow for scalable and high-quality designs.

- **Component Libraries:** Design tools often provide features for creating and managing libraries of reusable components, such as buttons, icons, and navigation menus.

- **Responsive Design Support:** Many modern design tools include features for designing responsive layouts, allowing designers to see how designs adapt to different screen sizes.

- **Interactivity:** Prototyping tools within design applications enable designers to add interactive elements, transitions, and animations to their designs.

- **Collaboration Features:** Web-based tools like Figma prioritize real-time collaboration, enabling designers and stakeholders to work together seamlessly.

d. Learning Web Design Tools:

- Learning web design tools is essential for web designers and UX professionals. Consider the following steps:

  - **Tutorials and Courses:** Explore online tutorials and courses specific to the tool you want to learn. Many educational platforms offer in-depth courses on popular design tools.

- **Official Documentation:** Refer to official documentation and user guides provided by the tool's creators.

- **Practice:** Hands-on practice is crucial. Start with small projects and gradually work your way up to more complex ones.

- **Online Communities:** Join online communities and forums related to the tool you're learning. These can be valuable for asking questions, sharing tips, and staying updated.

- **Collaborate:** Collaborate with other designers or professionals on projects to gain practical experience.

e. Staying Updated:

- The field of web design tools is continually evolving. Stay updated with new features, updates, and best practices by following official blogs, online forums, and industry news.

f. Choosing the Right Tool:

- The choice of web design tool depends on your specific needs, platform preferences, and team collaboration requirements. It's a good idea to try out different tools to see which one aligns best with your workflow.

In conclusion, web design tools are indispensable for web designers and UI/UX professionals. Familiarizing yourself with popular design tools like Adobe XD, Sketch, or Figma empowers you to create visually stunning designs, interactive prototypes, and collaborate effectively with others. Continuous learning, practice, and staying updated are essential to mastering these tools and enhancing your web design skills.

15. Web Hosting and Domain:

a. Web Hosting:

- **Web hosting** is the service of storing and serving website files, including HTML, CSS, JavaScript, images, and databases, on a server that is accessible over the internet. It makes websites accessible to users 24/7. Here's what you need to know:

i. Types of Web Hosting:

1. **Shared Hosting:** Websites share server resources with other websites on the same server. It's cost-effective but may have limitations on performance and customization.

2. **Virtual Private Server (VPS) Hosting:** A VPS is a virtualized server environment created within a physical server. It offers more control and resources than shared hosting.

3. **Dedicated Hosting:** You get an entire server for your website. This provides the highest level of

control, performance, and security but is also the most expensive.

4. **Cloud Hosting:** Resources are spread across multiple virtual servers, providing scalability and redundancy. It's suitable for websites with varying traffic loads.

5. **Managed WordPress Hosting:** Tailored for WordPress websites, this hosting type offers specialized support and optimization for WordPress CMS.

ii. Key Hosting Features:

- **Uptime:** Hosting providers typically offer uptime guarantees. Look for providers with high uptime percentages (99.9% or higher).

- **Bandwidth and Data Transfer:** Consider the amount of data your website will transfer monthly. Ensure the hosting plan accommodates your expected traffic.

- **Storage:** Hosting plans offer different storage capacities. Choose one that suits your website's size and content.

- **Server Location:** The physical location of the server can impact website speed and SEO. Select a server location that aligns with your target audience.

- **Scalability:** Choose a hosting plan that allows you to easily scale resources as your website grows.

- **Support:** Reliable customer support is essential. Ensure the hosting provider offers responsive support through various channels.

b. Domain Registration:

- A **domain name** is the web address that users enter in their browsers to access your website (e.g., www.example.com). Registering a domain is like obtaining a unique address for your website on the internet.

i. Domain Registration Process:

1. **Choose a Domain Name:** Select a unique, memorable, and brand-appropriate domain name for your website.

2. **Check Domain Availability:** Use domain registrars or hosting providers to check if your desired domain name is available.

3. **Select a Domain Registrar:** Choose a reputable domain registrar or hosting provider to register your domain. Popular registrars include GoDaddy, Namecheap, and Google Domains.

4. **Register the Domain:** Follow the registrar's instructions to complete the domain registration process. You'll need to provide contact information, and you may have the option to purchase additional services like domain privacy protection.

5. **Manage DNS Settings:** Configure the Domain Name System (DNS) settings to point your domain to your hosting server. This step ensures that visitors are directed to the correct web server when they enter your domain in their browsers.

ii. Domain Extensions:

- Domain names come with various **domain extensions** (also known as top-level domains or

TLDs), such as .com, .org, .net, .io, and many others. The choice of domain extension depends on your website's purpose and target audience.

- Country code TLDs (ccTLDs), like .uk for the United Kingdom or .ca for Canada, may be used to signify a specific geographic focus.

c. Choosing a Hosting Provider and Domain Registrar:

- Consider the following factors when selecting a hosting provider and domain registrar:

  - **Reputation:** Choose reputable companies with a track record of reliable service and good customer support.

  - **Pricing:** Compare pricing plans and consider any hidden costs or renewal fees.

  - **Customer Support:** Ensure that customer support is accessible and responsive, especially in case of technical issues.

- **Scalability:** Your hosting and domain registrar should accommodate your website's growth.

- **Security:** Look for providers that offer security features such as SSL certificates and data backups.

- **User Interface:** A user-friendly control panel can make managing your hosting and domain easier.

d. Domain and Hosting Integration:

- To make your website live, you'll need to connect your domain to your hosting account. This typically involves updating DNS records to point to your hosting server's IP address.

- Many hosting providers offer domain registration services, simplifying the integration process.

e. Renewal and Maintenance:

- Domains and hosting plans typically require renewal on an annual or monthly basis. Keep track of renewal dates to prevent disruptions to your website.

f. Website Building:

- Once your domain and hosting are in place, you can start building your website. You can use web design tools, content management systems, or code from scratch, depending on your skills and project requirements.

In conclusion, understanding web hosting and domain registration is essential for anyone involved in web development and website management. By selecting reliable hosting providers and domain registrars, configuring DNS settings, and considering factors like scalability and security, you can ensure a smooth and successful launch of your website on the internet.

16. Web Accessibility:

a. What is Web Accessibility:

- **Web accessibility** refers to the practice of designing and developing websites and web applications that can be used by all individuals, including those with disabilities. It aims to eliminate barriers and provide equal access to information and functionality.

- Web accessibility is not limited to users with specific disabilities; it benefits a broad range of users, including those with visual, auditory, motor, and cognitive impairments.

b. The Importance of Web Accessibility:

- Web accessibility is essential for the following reasons:

  - **Inclusivity:** It ensures that people with disabilities have equal access to digital content and services, promoting inclusivity.

- **Legal Compliance:** In many countries, there are legal requirements or standards that mandate web accessibility.

- **Improved User Experience:** Accessible websites are more user-friendly for everyone, leading to better user experiences.

- **Wider Audience Reach:** Accessible websites can reach a broader audience, including potential customers and clients.

c. Web Accessibility Standards:

- **Web Content Accessibility Guidelines (WCAG):** WCAG is the most widely recognized set of accessibility guidelines. It is developed and maintained by the World Wide Web Consortium (W3C). WCAG is organized into four principles, each with a set of success criteria:

  1. **Perceivable:** Information and user interface components must be presented in a way that is perceivable by all users, including those with disabilities.

2. **Operable:** User interface components and navigation must be operable by all users, including those who use assistive technologies.

3. **Understandable:** Information and operation of user interface must be understandable by all users, including those with cognitive disabilities.

4. **Robust:** Content must be robust enough to be reliably interpreted by a wide variety of user agents, including assistive technologies.

- **Levels of Conformance:** WCAG provides three levels of conformance: A (lowest), AA (mid-level), and AAA (highest). WCAG 2.0 and 2.1 are widely used, with WCAG 2.1 being the most recent version.

d. Key Accessibility Considerations:

- **Semantic HTML:** Use proper HTML elements to convey content structure and meaning. For example, use headings (h1, h2, etc.) to structure content hierarchically.

- **Keyboard Accessibility:** Ensure all functionality and interactive elements are operable using a keyboard alone, as some users rely on keyboard navigation.

- **Alternative Text:** Provide descriptive alt text for images and other non-text content to make them accessible to screen readers.

- **Captions and Transcripts:** Include captions for multimedia content (videos) and provide transcripts for audio content to assist users with hearing impairments.

- **Contrast and Visual Design:** Ensure sufficient contrast between text and background colors for readability. Avoid relying solely on color to convey information.

- **Form Accessibility:** Design accessible forms, including proper labeling and error messages. Ensure form fields are easy to navigate.

- **Focus Indicators:** Ensure that focus indicators (the visible outline around focused elements) are present and styled appropriately for keyboard navigation.

e. Testing and Evaluation:

- Regularly test your website for accessibility using a combination of automated accessibility testing tools and manual testing, which includes using screen readers and keyboard navigation.

- Consider involving users with disabilities in usability testing to get direct feedback on the accessibility of your website.

f. Resources for Learning and Implementation:

- The Web Accessibility Initiative (WAI) provides extensive resources, including the WCAG guidelines, techniques, and educational materials.

- Online courses and training programs, such as those offered by Coursera and edX, can provide in-depth knowledge and practical skills in web accessibility.

- Web accessibility tools and extensions, such as WAVE, axe, and screen readers like JAWS and NVDA, can help in testing and learning about web accessibility.

g. Ongoing Commitment:

- Web accessibility is an ongoing commitment. As web technologies evolve, it's crucial to keep your websites up to date with the latest accessibility standards and best practices.

In conclusion, web accessibility is a vital aspect of web design and development that ensures equal access to digital content and services for all users. Familiarizing yourself with web accessibility standards like WCAG, implementing best practices, and regularly testing your websites for accessibility will help create a more inclusive online environment that benefits everyone, regardless of their abilities or disabilities.

17. SEO Basics:

a. What is SEO:

- **Search Engine Optimization (SEO)** is the practice of optimizing websites and web content to improve their visibility in search engine results pages (SERPs). The primary goal of SEO is to attract more organic (non-paid) traffic by ranking higher in search engine listings.

- SEO involves various strategies and techniques to make a website more search engine-friendly and user-friendly.

b. Key SEO Principles:

- **Keyword Research:** Understand the keywords and phrases users enter into search engines to find content related to your website. Use tools like Google Keyword Planner or third-party tools to identify relevant keywords.

- **On-Page Optimization:** Optimize individual web pages by placing keywords strategically in page titles, headings, meta descriptions, and throughout the content. Ensure that the content is high-quality, valuable, and engaging.

- **Technical SEO:** Improve the technical aspects of your website, including site speed, mobile-friendliness, and crawlability. Use clean, semantic HTML code and XML sitemaps to assist search engines in indexing your site.

- **Backlinks:** Acquire high-quality backlinks from authoritative and relevant websites. Backlinks are seen as a vote of confidence in your content and can positively impact your rankings.

- **User Experience (UX):** Provide a positive user experience by creating intuitive navigation, clear calls to action, and fast-loading pages. A good user experience can indirectly improve your SEO.

- **Content Marketing:** Develop a content strategy that focuses on creating informative, valuable, and shareable content. High-quality content can attract natural backlinks and engage users.

c. On-Page SEO:

- On-page SEO refers to optimization efforts conducted directly on individual web pages to improve their search engine ranking. Key elements of on-page SEO include:

    - **Keyword Usage:** Place relevant keywords in strategic locations, such as titles, headings, content, and image alt attributes.

    - **Meta Tags:** Optimize meta titles and descriptions to accurately represent the content and encourage click-throughs from search results.

    - **Content Quality:** Create well-researched, comprehensive, and unique content that addresses users' needs and questions.

    - **URL Structure:** Use descriptive and user-friendly URLs that include keywords when appropriate.

    - **Internal Linking:** Create a logical and organized internal linking structure to help users navigate your site and improve the flow of PageRank.

- **Image Optimization:** Compress images for faster loading times and use descriptive file names and alt tags.

d. Off-Page SEO:

- Off-page SEO refers to actions taken outside your website to improve its search engine ranking. Key components include:

  - **Link Building:** Acquire backlinks from authoritative and relevant websites through guest posting, outreach, and content promotion.

  - **Social Signals:** Engage on social media platforms to increase brand visibility and potentially attract traffic and backlinks.

  - **Online Reputation Management:** Monitor and manage online reviews and mentions to maintain a positive online reputation.

e. Technical SEO:

- Technical SEO focuses on optimizing the technical aspects of your website to improve its search engine visibility. Important technical SEO elements include:

- **Website Speed:** Ensure fast loading times by optimizing images, enabling browser caching, and using a content delivery network (CDN).

- **Mobile Optimization:** Design your website to be responsive and mobile-friendly to cater to users on various devices.

- **XML Sitemaps:** Create and submit XML sitemaps to help search engines discover and index your website's pages.

- **Schema Markup:** Implement structured data markup (schema.org) to enhance search engine understanding of your content and improve rich snippet displays.

- **Crawlability:** Ensure that search engine bots can efficiently crawl and index your website. Use robots.txt and sitemap.xml files to guide crawlers.

f. SEO Tools:

- Various SEO tools can help you analyze, track, and optimize your website's performance. Examples include Google Analytics, Google Search Console, Moz, SEMrush, Ahrefs, and more.

g. Continuous Monitoring and Optimization:

- SEO is an ongoing process. Regularly monitor your website's performance, rankings, and user behavior through analytics tools. Make necessary adjustments and optimizations based on data and changing search engine algorithms.

h. Learning Resources:

- SEO is a continually evolving field. Stay updated with industry news and best practices by following reputable SEO blogs, forums, and taking online courses or certifications.

In conclusion, understanding the basics of SEO is essential for web designers and developers to create websites that are not only visually appealing but also search engine-friendly. By implementing on-page and off-page optimization techniques, technical SEO best practices, and continuously monitoring your website's performance, you can improve your site's visibility in search engine results and attract more organic traffic.

18. Continuous Learning in Web Design:

a. The Importance of Continuous Learning:

- **Rapid Technological Evolution:** The digital landscape, including web design, is constantly evolving. New technologies, frameworks, and design trends emerge regularly. Staying current is essential to remain competitive.

- **User Expectations:** Users expect modern, user-friendly, and visually appealing websites. Meeting these expectations requires keeping up with design and usability standards.

- **SEO and Accessibility:** Search engine algorithms change, and web accessibility standards evolve. Continuous learning ensures that your websites are optimized for search engines and accessible to all users.

- **Innovation:** Learning keeps your creative juices flowing. Exposure to new ideas and approaches can lead to innovative design solutions.

b. Strategies for Continuous Learning:

- **1. Online Courses and Tutorials:** Enroll in online courses and tutorials offered by platforms like Coursera, Udemy, edX, and LinkedIn Learning. These courses cover various aspects of web design, from coding to user experience.

- **2. Books and Ebooks:** Invest in web design books and ebooks. There are publications on topics like responsive design, UX/UI design, and coding languages that provide valuable insights.

- **3. Webinars and Workshops:** Attend webinars and workshops conducted by industry experts. These events often focus on emerging trends and technologies.

- **4. Blogs and Newsletters:** Follow web design blogs and subscribe to newsletters from reputable sources. These publications provide updates on design trends, tools, and best practices.

- **5. Forums and Online Communities:** Join web design forums and online communities like Stack Overflow, Smashing Magazine, and

Reddit's web design subreddits. Engaging in discussions and seeking advice from peers can be invaluable.

- **6. Design Challenges:** Participate in design challenges and competitions. These exercises push you out of your comfort zone and encourage creativity.

- **7. Industry Conferences:** Attend web design conferences and networking events. These gatherings offer opportunities to learn from experts and connect with fellow professionals.

- **8. Online Platforms and Tools:** Experiment with new design tools and platforms like Figma, Sketch, and Adobe XD. Learning these tools can enhance your efficiency and design capabilities.

- **9. Open Source Contributions:** Contribute to open source web design projects. Collaborating with others on projects can teach you valuable teamwork and coding skills.

c. Staying Updated with Trends:

- Regularly read design-focused magazines, websites, and social media accounts to stay informed about the latest design trends, color schemes, typography, and visual styles.

- Follow influential designers and design agencies on platforms like Behance, Dribbble, and Instagram to discover cutting-edge designs and inspiration.

d. Building a Portfolio:

- Implement what you've learned in real projects and build a diverse portfolio that showcases your skills. A strong portfolio is essential for attracting clients and job opportunities.

e. Networking:

- Attend meetups, conferences, and webinars to network with other professionals in the field. Building a network can lead to collaborative opportunities and knowledge sharing.

f. Adapting to New Technologies:

- Stay updated with the latest web development technologies, such as new versions of HTML, CSS, and JavaScript, as well as emerging technologies like WebAssembly and Progressive Web Apps (PWAs).

g. Experimentation and Personal Projects:

- Don't hesitate to experiment with new design techniques, tools, and ideas in personal projects. These projects allow you to test your skills and creativity without client constraints.

h. Time Management:

- Allocate dedicated time for learning. Schedule regular periods for reading, taking courses, and experimenting with new technologies.

i. Embrace Failure:

- Not everything you try will succeed. Embrace failure as a learning opportunity and don't be afraid to pivot and try new approaches.

j. Mentorship:

- Seek mentorship from experienced web designers or developers. Mentors can provide guidance, share their knowledge, and help you navigate your career path.

In conclusion, continuous learning is an indispensable part of a successful web design career. The web design field is dynamic, and to stay competitive, you must keep pace with emerging trends, technologies, and best practices. Commit to ongoing education, experimentation, and networking to ensure your skills remain relevant and your designs continue to meet the evolving needs and expectations of users and clients.

19. Practice and Projects:

a. The Significance of Practice:

- **Hands-on Experience:** Practical application of your knowledge is vital. It allows you to turn theoretical concepts into tangible skills.

- **Problem Solving:** Real-world projects present various challenges. By solving these problems, you gain problem-solving skills that are valuable in the industry.

- **Portfolio Building:** Projects serve as portfolio pieces that showcase your abilities to potential employers or clients. A strong portfolio is often more compelling than academic qualifications alone.

- **Confidence Building:** The more you practice, the more confident you become in your abilities. Confidence is key when working on client projects or in a professional environment.

b. Personal Projects:

- **1. Choose a Focus:** Start with a specific area of web design or development that interests you, such as front-end development, UX/UI design, or back-end development.

- **2. Define Goals:** Set clear goals for your project. What skills do you want to develop or showcase? What kind of website or application do you want to create?

- **3. Plan and Research:** Plan your project thoroughly, including design sketches, wireframes, and technology choices. Research best practices and gather resources.

- **4. Start Small:** If you're new to web design, begin with small, manageable projects. As you gain confidence and skills, gradually take on more complex challenges.

- **5. Continuously Learn:** Use personal projects as opportunities to learn. Don't be afraid to explore new tools, frameworks, or technologies.

- **6. Seek Feedback:** Share your work with peers, mentors, or online communities. Constructive feedback can help you improve.

- **7. Document Your Work:** Keep a record of your projects, including the problems you encountered and how you solved them. This documentation can be valuable for future reference.

c. Freelance Work:

- **1. Building a Portfolio:** Freelance work is an excellent way to build your portfolio. Start by taking on smaller projects that align with your skills.

- **2. Networking:** Connect with potential clients through freelancing platforms like Upwork, Freelancer, or Fiverr. Attend networking events and engage with local businesses.

- **3. Contracts and Agreements:** Always have clear contracts and agreements in place with clients. Outline project scope, timelines, payment terms, and expectations.

- **4. Client Communication:** Effective communication is essential. Understand your client's needs, ask questions, and provide regular updates on project progress.

- **5. Time Management:** Freelancing requires excellent time management skills. Balance multiple projects while meeting deadlines.

- **6. Pricing:** Determine your pricing strategy based on factors like your experience, the project's complexity, and market rates.

- **7. Upskilling:** Freelance work may expose you to various client requirements. Use these opportunities to expand your skill set.

d. Continuous Learning:

- Keep learning while working on personal projects or freelance assignments. Stay updated with the latest trends, technologies, and best practices in the web design and development field.

- Invest time in self-study, online courses, tutorials, and workshops to expand your knowledge and skills.

e. Professionalism:

- Whether working on personal projects or freelancing, maintain professionalism in your interactions with clients, peers, and collaborators. Reputation and referrals are essential in freelancing.

f. Perseverance:

- Building a successful career in web design or development takes time. Be patient, stay motivated, and continue practicing and learning.

g. Contributions to Open Source:

- Consider contributing to open-source projects related to web design or development. This not only helps you practice but also gives back to the community.

In summary, practice and personal projects are essential for honing your web design and development skills. They provide you with practical experience, help you build a strong portfolio, and prepare you for freelance work or a career in the industry. By setting clear goals, continuously learning, and approaching projects with dedication and professionalism, you can progress and thrive in the field of web design and development.

20. Feedback and Critique in Web Design:

a. The Significance of Feedback:

- **Objective Evaluation:** Feedback provides an objective evaluation of your work from a different perspective. It helps identify areas for improvement that you might overlook.

- **Learning Opportunity:** Constructive criticism offers an opportunity for learning and growth. It can introduce you to new techniques, best practices, and design trends.

- **Validation:** Positive feedback reinforces your strengths and boosts confidence, motivating you to continue improving.

- **Client Satisfaction:** Understanding and addressing client feedback is crucial for client satisfaction and project success.

b. Sources of Feedback:

- **1. Experienced Designers:** Seek feedback from experienced designers or mentors who can offer expert insights and guidance.

- **2. Peer Reviews:** Engage in peer reviews with fellow designers or classmates. They can provide fresh perspectives and practical suggestions.

- **3. Online Communities:** Participate in design communities and forums, such as Behance, Dribbble, or specialized web design subreddits. Share your work and actively critique others' work to receive reciprocal feedback.

- **4. Workshops and Courses:** If you're taking web design courses or workshops, leverage the feedback provided by instructors.

- **5. Clients and Users:** Solicit feedback from clients and end-users to understand how well your design meets their needs and expectations.

c. How to Seek Effective Feedback:

- **1. Be Specific:** When requesting feedback, be clear about what aspects of your design you'd like to be reviewed. Are you interested in overall aesthetics, usability, or specific design elements?

- **2. Provide Context:** Offer context about the project, its goals, and the target audience. Understanding the project's objectives helps reviewers provide relevant feedback.

- **3. Ask Open-Ended Questions:** Encourage constructive feedback by asking open-ended questions. For example, "What could be improved in the navigation menu to enhance user experience?"

- **4. Be Open to Criticism:** Be open-minded and receptive to criticism. Remember that feedback is meant to help you improve, not to criticize your abilities.

- **5. Consider Diverse Perspectives:** Seek feedback from a variety of sources with different backgrounds and experiences. This diversity can provide well-rounded insights.

- **6. Separate Personal from Professional:** Avoid taking feedback personally. Focus on the design, not your self-worth.

d. Evaluating and Implementing Feedback:

- **1. Analyze Feedback:** Take time to analyze the feedback you receive. Identify recurring themes and prioritize areas that need improvement.

- **2. Decide on Changes:** Determine which feedback you will implement. Not all suggestions may align with your design vision or project requirements.

- **3. Iterate:** Make revisions based on the feedback and critique. Repeat the process of seeking feedback and refining your work until you achieve your desired outcome.

e. Giving Constructive Feedback:

- When providing feedback to others, offer constructive criticism that is specific, actionable, and respectful. Point out what works well and provide suggestions for improvement.

f. Participating in Design Communities:

- Engage actively in design communities and forums. Share your work, provide thoughtful critiques, and engage in discussions to establish a presence and build professional relationships.

g. Continuous Improvement:

- Use feedback and critique as a continuous improvement tool. As you grow as a designer, your ability to provide and receive feedback will also improve.

h. Learning from Critique:

- Critique sessions are a valuable opportunity to learn from others and develop a critical eye for design. The more you engage in the critique process, the more refined your design skills will become.

In summary, feedback and critique are essential elements of professional growth in web design. They provide opportunities for learning, improvement, and exposure to diverse perspectives. By actively seeking feedback, remaining open to constructive criticism, and participating in design communities, you can refine your skills, create more effective designs, and ultimately become a more proficient web designer.

Conclusion:

Congratulations on completing this comprehensive beginner's guide to web design! You've embarked on a rewarding journey that opens up a world of creativity, problem-solving, and digital innovation. To summarize, here are the key takeaways:

1. **Learn the Fundamentals:** Start with HTML and CSS, the building blocks of web design.

2. **Select the Right Tools:** Choose text editors or IDEs like Visual Studio Code at [https://code.visualstudio.com/], Sublime Text at [https://www.sublimetext.com/], or Atom at [https://atom.io/] to code efficiently.

3. **Master Responsive Design:** Ensure your websites look great on all devices and screen sizes by understanding responsive web design principles.

4. **Typography Matters:** Explore typography principles using resources like Google Fonts at

[https://fonts.google.com/] to choose and use fonts effectively.

5. **Color Harmony:** Grasp the basics of color theory from sources like Adobe Color at [https://color.adobe.com/] to create harmonious color schemes.

6. **Layout and Grids:** Study layout principles and grid systems for organized and visually appealing web pages.

7. **Images and Multimedia:** Optimize images and incorporate multimedia elements effectively.

8. **Navigation:** Design intuitive navigation menus and site structures for improved user experience.

9. **UI and UX:** Familiarize yourself with UI and UX principles for user-friendly designs.

10. **Coding Practice:** Regularly practice coding to reinforce your skills and take on small to large projects.

11. **Frameworks and Libraries:** Consider using frameworks and libraries to streamline your development process.

12. **Responsive Web Design Frameworks:** Explore responsive web design frameworks like Flexbox and CSS Grid for fluid layouts.

13. **Content Management Systems (CMS):** Learn to use popular CMS platforms like WordPress, Joomla, or Drupal for efficient website creation.

14. **Web Design Tools:** Familiarize yourself with design tools like Adobe XD, Sketch, or Figma for creating mockups and prototypes.

15. **Web Hosting and Domain:** Understand how to host a website and register domain names with providers like Bluehost or Namecheap.

16. **Web Accessibility:** Prioritize web accessibility standards (WCAG) to ensure inclusive websites that cater to all users.

17. **SEO Basics:** Get acquainted with fundamental SEO principles to improve your site's visibility in search engines.

18. **Continuous Learning:** Web design is ever-evolving, so stay updated with the latest trends, technologies, and design practices. Visit reputable resources like Smashing Magazine, WebAIM, W3Schools, and Coursera.

19. **Practice and Projects:** Apply what you've learned by working on personal projects or taking on freelance work for practical experience.

20. **Feedback and Critique:** Seek feedback from experienced designers and participate in design communities or forums for constructive criticism.

Remember, web design is not just about creating websites; it's about crafting exceptional digital experiences. Continue honing your skills, stay curious, and embrace the ever-changing landscape of web design. Your journey has just begun, and with dedication and creativity, you'll be well on your way to becoming a proficient web designer. Best of luck!

Printed in Great Britain
by Amazon

40369845R00076